read write

Read the sentences then write yes or no by each picture.

KV-193-267

Wex has two biscuits.

_____

Humpty Dumpty is on the wall.

_____

The King's Men have red hats.

_____

Vaz can ride the bike.

_____

Finish drawing the pictures and colour them.
Then match each picture to the correct word.

nail   map   robot   hammer   house   rat   man

Write **sa** in the spaces.

Which castles have the word **sand** on them?

Colour their flags.

Which other words can you see?

_ _ nd

_ _ d

_ _ ck

_ _ nd

_ _ t

_ _ nd

_ _ ck

_ _ nd

talk

I spy with my little eye,
something beginning with...

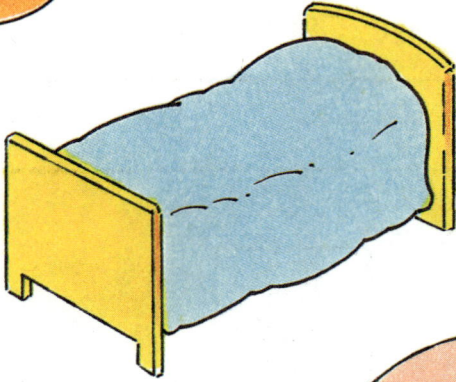

4

Find the hidden words.
You can go across or down.

puzzle

when
up
there
gone
could
would
turned
stop
plate
her
own
drink
creature

o	w	n	p	y	w	t	z
x	d	h	l	s	o	u	p
c	r	e	a	t	u	r	e
g	i	r	t	o	l	n	q
o	n	p	e	p	d	e	w
n	k	c	o	u	l	d	h
e	r	s	t	h	e	r	e
m	s	g	i	o	i	m	n

Draw a line to join the words below that have the
same rhyming sound.

good   Mike   wall   down

fall   come   wood   Ben

then   some   bike   crown

5

Look at the pictures.
Tell the story.

In each row, colour the picture that is the same as the first one.

puzzle

colour draw

Finish all the patterns across the page and colour the pictures.

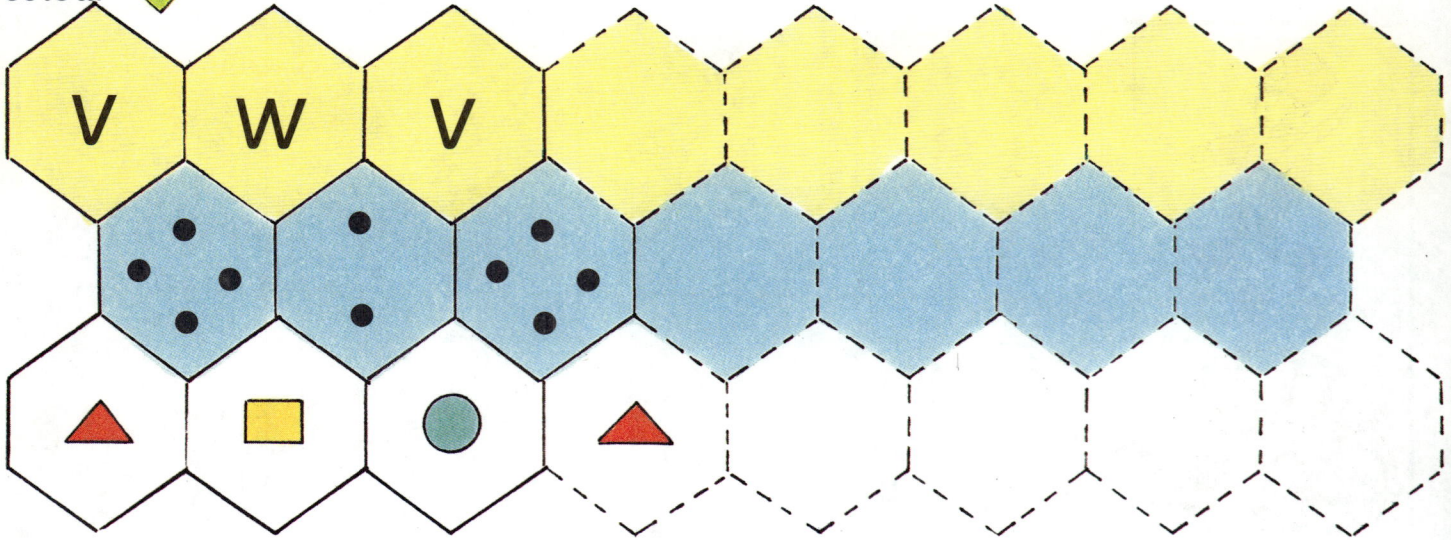

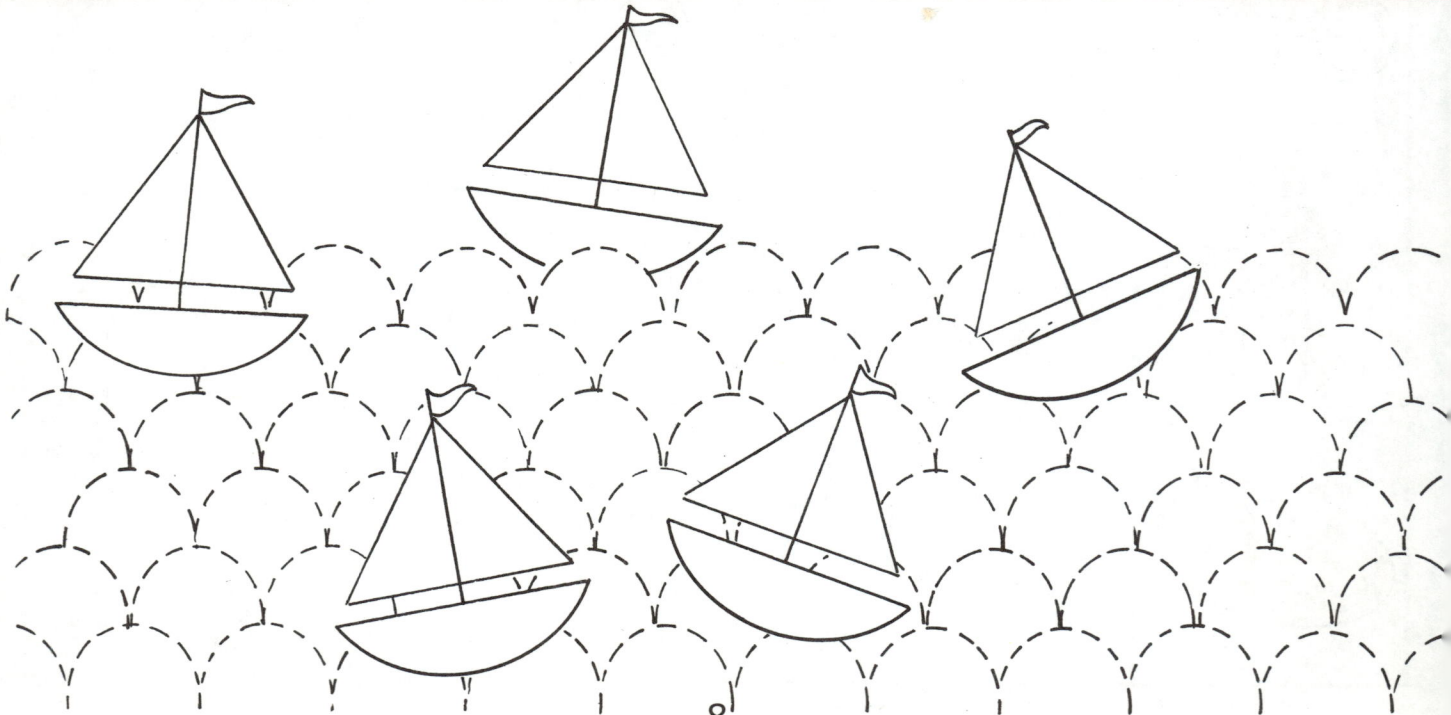

read

draw

Draw a circle round the word that goes in each space.

The crown _____ on the octopus.
(put, **is**, are)

Jenny _____ two biscuits.
(**has**, from, gone)

Troll is sitting _____ Humpty.
(must, **with**, home)

The pirate _____ over the sand.
(would, some, **walked**)

Imp was scared _____ the snake.
(**of**, my, on)

The treasure was _____ the tree.
(like, **in**, more)

9

Find at least 6 differences between these pictures, then colour the bottom one.

10

puzzle

Draw a line to join the two parts of each picture.

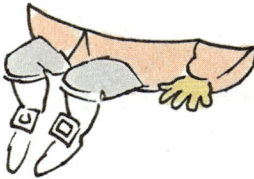

Use the words below to fill in the spaces on Humpty Dumpty's wall.

no_ _	na_ _	nee_	ne_ _
	ni_ _	h_ _	m_
_y	mo_ _	no_	mos_
	r_ _	ma_ _	m_ d_
mu_ _	h_ld	he_ _	t_l_
	_ _de	n_ _d	_ery
w_ _ _	_ome	_ith	h_r_

now note name my made need next
held help must make most him nice
move me ran rode very want with
home need told here

Help Wex to find the door to the flying saucer.

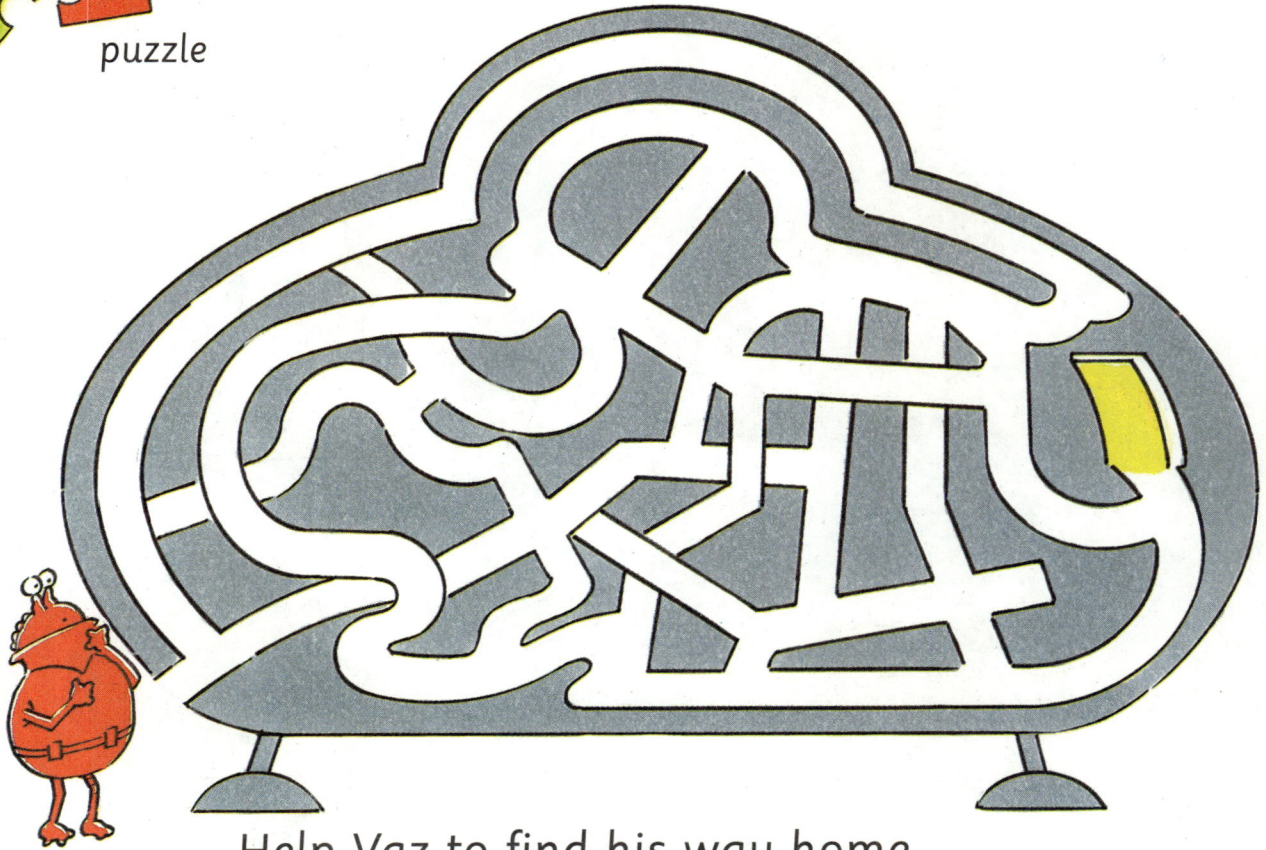

puzzle

Help Vaz to find his way home.

read
write

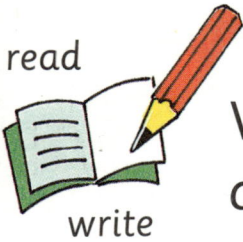

Write the correct word by each picture.

Vaz Wex Ben Jenny robot dogs
cars bike biscuits drink tree

_____

_____

_____

_____

_____

_____

_____

_____

_____

_____

_____

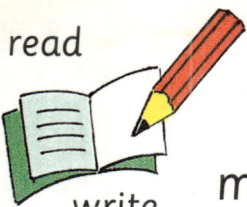
read
write

Draw a line to the words that match and write each word again.

my	made	_____
his	have	_____
made	more	_____
her	how	_____
me	my	_____
more	his	_____
many	her	_____
have	me	_____
how	has	_____
has	many	_____

match

Match the correct word to the picture.

frog

house

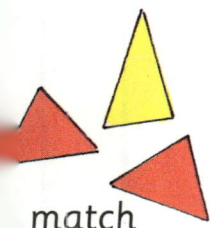

beach

biscuit

crown

hill

drink

Talk about the picture.

What are Ben and Jenny doing?
Who can you see hiding?

Finish the patterns round the edge of the picture.

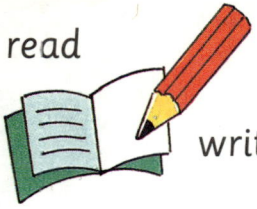
read

write

Read the sentences and fill in the correct word.

house   map   wall   plates

The strange man
looks at the _____.

The king breaks two _____.

The robot
disappears by the _____.

Wex and Vaz
are sitting on the _____.

match

colour

Say the beginning sounds. Match them to the correct pictures. Colour the pictures.

sh ch th pl wh sn kn

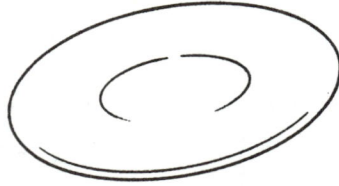
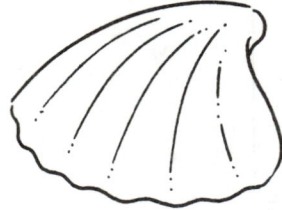
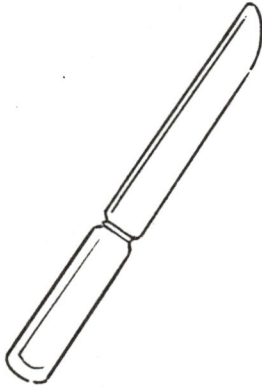
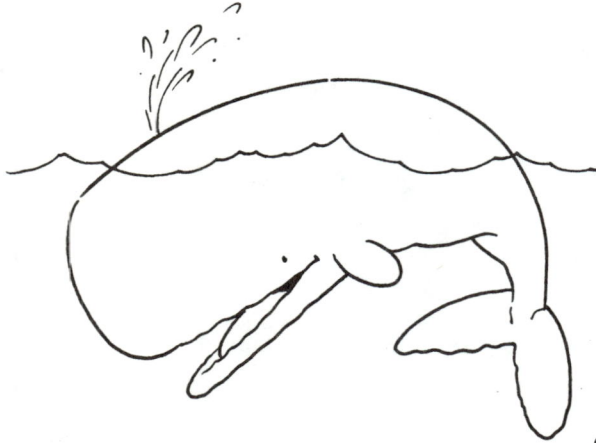

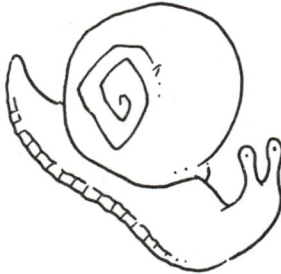
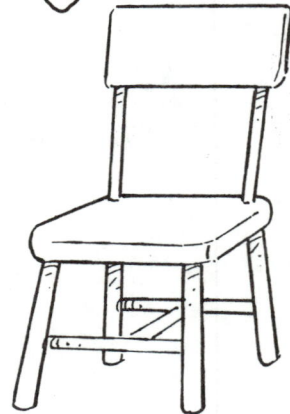
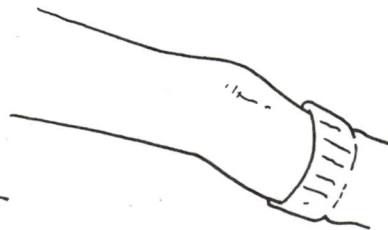

18

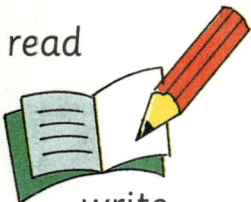

read
write

Read the words and write the sentence underneath.

The King's Men were riding bikes.

_____

Vaz and Wex had some tea.

_____

Humpty Dumpty rode in the car.

_____

Jenny saw a strange creature.

_____

Ben could not see Mike.

_____

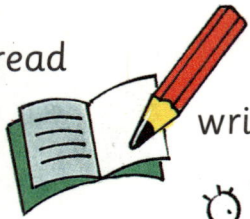

Match the correct object to each character.

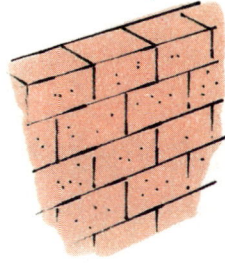

Match the words and write them again.

all	are	_____
went	where	_____
are	way	_____
where	came	_____
be	but	_____
but	went	_____
was	be	_____
way	was	_____
by	all	_____
came	by	_____

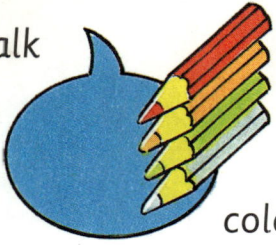

Talk about the picture.
What might happen next?
Colour the picture any way you like.

 read write

Fill in the missing words.

Humpty   robots   biscuits   elephant

_____ Dumpty fell off

the _____ .

The_____ had

some _____ .

Jenny   Vaz   up   scared   hill   car

_____ was _____ of the _____ .

_____ and Wex rode

_____ the _____ .

Join the dots and colour the picture.

Who is sitting on the wall?
Can you say the nursery rhyme?

Vaz and Wex come from another planet.
What do you think it looks like?

Write the beginning sound for each picture.